W9-ALM-560

GIFTED & TALENTED®

*To develop
your child's gifts
and talents*

Kitchen Science Experiments

For Ages 6–8

By Barbara Saffer, Ph.D.

Illustrations by Leo Abbett

LOWELL HOUSE JUVENILE

LOS ANGELES

NTC/Contemporary Publishing Group

For my helpers, Chelsea and Brandon
—B.S.

Published by Lowell House
A division of NTC/Contemporary Publishing Group, Inc.
4255 West Touhy Avenue, Lincolnwood (Chicago), Illinois 60712 U.S.A.

Managing Director and Publisher: Jack Artenstein
Director of Publishing Services: Rena Copperman
Editorial Director: Brenda Pope-Ostrow
Project Editor: Amy Hansen
Typesetter: Carolyn Wendt

Lowell House books can be purchased at special discounts
when ordered in bulk for premiums and special sales.
Contact Customer Service at the address above,
or call 1-800-323-4900.

Printed and bound in the United States of America

Library of Congress Catalog Card Number: 99-76527

ISBN: 0-7373-0374-3

RCP 10 9 8 7 6 5 4 3 2 1

Contents

Note to Parents

This book won't just ask your child to learn facts about science; this book will ask her to *do* science and think about how it works. What's more, once your child learns how to think, she will be developing the wisdom she will use through the rest of her life. This is the reason that thinking skills are stressed in classrooms throughout the country. And it is the reason that our series of Gifted & Talented® materials is based on developing these important life tools.

Gifted & Talented Kitchen Science Experiments offers excursions into everyday **biology, chemistry,** and **physics**. You will enjoy working with your child as she explores the properties of a plastic bag, creates invisible ink, or builds a musical instrument from a drinking straw. Discuss each experiment before you begin. You may want to talk about some of the science concepts in this book and skip over parts she is not ready for. There is no need for your child to finish every activity in the book. Work with her to pick and choose the ones appropriate for both of you. And, of course, encourage her to ask questions. Key terms, defined in the Glossary at the back of the book, are set in **boldface** type in each experiment.

Each of the experiments has its own set of questions, which are designed to promote the development of critical- and creative-thinking skills. With these questions, you'll be encouraging your child to go beyond a response of "That was neat!" to an understanding of how the process works and where it fits into our world. These questions will help develop such skills as knowledge and recall, comprehension, deduction, inference, sequencing, prediction, classification, analyzing, problem solving, and creative expansion.

And finally, when you do ask a question, give your child a moment to think before she answers. Try counting to 10 before you offer any suggestions. You'd be surprised how many parents and teachers ask a question and then jump right in and answer the question themselves. Suggested answers are provided at the back of the book.

Gifted & Talented Kitchen Science Experiments has been written and endorsed by educators. This book will benefit any child who is curious, imaginative, excited by the world, and eager to learn.

Introduction

You may not realize it, but science is all around you. If you put water in the freezer, it turns into ice. When you leave a banana on the counter, it ripens. If you overbake cookies, they get hard. These are all examples of science at work.

Scientists want to know how and why things happen. To find the answers to their questions, scientists use a procedure called the *scientific method*. This consists of five steps. An example will show you how it works.

Step 1 Ask a question.
Question: If a person places 10 substances into a freezer, will they all freeze at the same rate?

Step 2 Try to guess the answer. Scientists call such a guess a *hypothesis.*
Hypothesis: All 10 substances will freeze at the same rate.

Step 3 To check the hypothesis, set up a test or experiment.
Experiment: Put ⅛ cup of each of the following substances into an ice cube tray, one substance per compartment: apple juice, grape juice, lemon juice, ketchup, mayonnaise, mustard, pancake syrup, spaghetti sauce, vinegar, and water. Place a toothpick into each substance.

Put the ice cube tray into the freezer compartment of a refrigerator. Check the tray every 30 minutes. When you can lift a substance with the toothpick, the substance is frozen.

Step 4 Observe and record the rate at which the substances freeze.
Observations: The substances freeze at the following rates:*

  Water—1 hour plus a little
  Apple juice, grape juice, and lemon juice—2 hours
  Spaghetti sauce and vinegar—2 hours plus a little
  Mayonnaise and mustard—3 hours
  Ketchup and pancake syrup—4 hours

* The exact freezing times may vary, depending on the temperature in the freezer.

Step 5 Draw a conclusion. What does the experiment show?

Conclusion: Different substances freeze at different rates. In this example, the results don't agree with the hypothesis. The hypothesis is wrong. The scientist would have to form a new hypothesis and do another experiment to check it.

Actually, scientists know that different substances freeze at different rates. Plain water freezes quickly because it doesn't have other particles *dissolved,* or spread out, in it. The other substances tested are made of water and assorted particles. They freeze at different rates, depending on the kind and number of particles they contain. After many years of performing these experiments, scientists can now look up the freezing rates of different substances in scientific books.

The experiments in this book demonstrate scientific principles that were discovered using the scientific method. None of the experiments require exotic equipment; in fact, you probably have most of what you need at home. If not, you should be able to find the things you need at a grocery store.

In science, it's important to set up and observe experiments carefully. This often requires measuring things: size, weight, volume, time, temperature, and so on. To make accurate measurements, scientists use special instruments such as rulers, scales, measuring spoons, measuring cups, clocks, thermometers, and so forth. If you do an experiment that requires measurements, use the proper equipment, and measure as carefully as you can.

Converting to Metric Equivalents

Use this chart if you need to convert a U.S. unit of measure to its metric system equivalent. For example: If an experiment calls for 2 tablespoons water and you need to measure the water using milliliters, multiply 2 by 14.8. You need 29.6 milliliters water to complete the experiment.

IF YOU HAVE	BUT YOU NEED	MULTIPLY BY
inches	centimeters	2.54
feet	meters	0.305
pounds	kilograms	0.45
ounces	milliliters	30.0
tablespoons	milliliters	14.8
teaspoons	milliliters	4.9
cups	milliliters	236.6
pints	liters	0.47
quarts	liters	0.95
gallons	liters	3.78

This book is filled with experiments that are fun for kids and adults to do together. Not every experiment will appeal to every kid, so start with something that interests you and follow these guidelines as you go to work:

1. Read all the instructions.
2. Gather the necessary materials.
3. Follow the directions carefully. If the experiment has a part that requires special adult supervision—such as someone to handle boiling water—the experiment will display this symbol: **! Adult Help Required**
4. Make accurate observations.
5. Pay attention to what is happening in the experiment.
6. Ask questions about parts of the experiment that you don't understand and discuss the results with an adult.
7. Never eat or drink any part of the experiment unless the instructions say you may do so. Because this is a kitchen science book, there are some experiments that are good to eat. These experiments will have this symbol next to them: **YUM!**
8. Clean up after the experiment is done.

Sometimes an experiment doesn't turn out the way you expected, or the way it is described in "What Happened." If your experiment doesn't work, try again. Now get started and have fun!

Pronunciation Guide

acetic (uh-SEET-ik)
allergic (uhl-ER-jik)
amino (uh-MEEN-oh)
ascorbic (uh-SKORB-ik)
Bernoulli (ber-NOOL-ee)
caboche (kah-BOSH)
casein (KAY-seen)
centrifugal (sen-TRIFF-uh-gul)
centripetal (sen-TRIP-ih-tal)
corrode (kuh-RODE)
dehydrate (dee-HI-drate)
desalination (DEE-sal-in-AY-shun)
diffusion (diff-FYOO-zhun)
drought (DROWT)

evaporates (ee-VAP-or-ates)
ferment (fer-MENT)
fungi (FUN-ji)
gliadin (GLY-ah-din)
gluten (GLOO-ten)
glutenin (GLOO-ten-in)
hypothesis (hi-POTH-eh-sis)
indicator (IN-dih-kate-er)
inertia (in-ER-sha)
molecules (MOLL-eh-kyools),
nucleic (new-KLAY-ik)
optical illusion (OP-tih-kul
    ill-LOO-zhun)
osmosis (os-MOH-sis)

oxide (OCKS-ide)
polyethylene (pahl-ee-ETH-ih-leen)
polymers (PAHL-ih-mers)
preservatives (preh-ZERV-a-tivs)
repels (reh-PELLS)
saturated (SATCH-er-ate-ed)
sodium bicarbonate (SO-dee-um
    bi-KAR-bun-ate)
solution (suh-LOO-shun)
sulfuric (sull-FYOOR-ik)
surface tension (SIR-fiss TEN-shun)
thaumatropes (THO-ma-tropes)
translucent (trans-LOOSE-ent)
whey (HWAY)

Puncture the Plastic Bag

If you push a pencil through a water-filled plastic bag, will the bag leak?

Background:

Plastics are strong, light, man-made materials. They're used to make bicycle helmets, soda bottles, car bumpers, flower pots, eating utensils, sandwich bags, and thousands of other items. Plastics are made of chemicals called **polymers**. Polymers are large, chainlike **molecules,** or particles. They're made of many smaller molecules attached together. Plastic bags are made of a polymer called *polyethylene*.

What You'll Need:

- zipper-top plastic sandwich bag
- water
- sink
- three sharp pencils

What to Do:

1. Fill a zipper-top plastic sandwich bag with water and seal it.

2. Holding the bag over a sink, carefully push a sharp pencil into one side of the bag and out the other. Does water leak out around the pencil?

3. Carefully push two more sharp pencils through the bag. Does water leak out around the pencils?

4. Remove the pencils. What happens?

What Happened:

When polyethylene plastic is punctured, its molecules *shrink,* or pull together a little. When you poked pencils through the plastic bag, the polyethylene shrunk around the pencils and closed off the holes. Therefore, water didn't leak out of the bag. When you pulled the pencils out of the bag, the holes were too large to close off. Therefore, water poured out of the bag.

One Step Further:

Fill another zipper-top plastic sandwich bag with water and seal it. Stick the tip of a small pin into the plastic bag and remove it. Does the bag leak?

Questions:

1. Can you name some items, other than those named above, that are made of plastic?

2. Rubber is a stretchy polymer that *repels,* or keeps out, water. Can you guess which green plant is used to make rubber? What is rubber used for?

3. Many people recycle plastic bottles and plastic bags. What does *recycle* mean? Can other household items be recycled?

4. A German chemist named Karl Ziegler invented polyethylene in 1953. How would you figure out how long ago that was?

5. Pretend that you've invented a material with useful new features. What can your material do? What is it used for? What is it called?

Clay Dough

Can you make sculptures out of flour dough?

Background:

Wheat flour, commonly used for baking, contains starch and **proteins**. The proteins are called *glutenin* and *gliadin*. When wheat flour is mixed with water, the proteins form a firm, stretchy substance called *gluten*.

What You'll Need:

- large bowl
- measuring cups
- measuring spoons
- mixing spoon
- 1¼ cups all-purpose flour
- ¾ cup salt
- 2 teaspoons cream of tartar
- ½ cup water
- 4 teaspoons vegetable oil
- wax paper
- flat surface
- paints or markers (optional)

What to Do:

1. In a large bowl, mix together 1¼ cups flour, ¾ cup salt, and 2 teaspoons cream of tartar.

2. Slowly add ½ cup water and 4 teaspoons vegetable oil. Mix the ingredients, blending them into dough.

3. Knead the dough with your hands until it stiffens and forms clay. If the clay is too soft, add a little flour. If the clay is too sticky, add a little vegetable oil. DO NOT EAT THE CLAY.

4. Place a large piece of wax paper on a flat surface, and put the clay on the wax paper. Make some sculptures with the clay, like fruit bowls, apples, bananas, pears, and so on.

5. Leave the sculptures in the open air for a few days, to dry and harden. Paint them or color them with markers if you like.

What Happened:

When flour and water are mixed, they form dough. Mixing and kneading the dough helps form a protein in flour called *gluten*. Scientists think that gluten is formed when other proteins, which are already in wheat, are mixed with liquid and kneaded together. Gluten gives dough a firm, claylike texture. Cream of tartar makes the dough smooth, and vegetable oil makes it creamy. The dough can then be molded into sculptures. When the sculptures dry in the open air, the water **evaporates,** or escapes into the air. The sculptures then become dry and hard.

One Step Further:

Try your hand at pea sculptures. Soak dried peas in water for several hours, until they soften. Using toothpicks as building elements, and softened peas as connectors, construct houses, dolls, and other shapes. Let your sculptures sit in the open air for a few days, until the peas dry out. The peas will shrink and hold the toothpicks in place.

Questions:

1. Do you think your clay sculptures would dry more quickly in a hot place or a cold place? Why?

2. What do you think wheat flour is made from? How do you think it's made?

3. Where do you think the clay used by pottery makers comes from?

4. Cake batter is made with flour, water, and other ingredients. Why shouldn't the batter be overmixed?

5. Some people are *allergic* to, or get sick from, wheat flour. What shouldn't they eat? What could they eat instead?

Candy Crystals

Can you make candy crystals from a sugar solution?

Adult Help Required

Background:

All substances are made of tiny particles called **atoms**. In crystals, the atoms are arranged in a particular pattern, and they form a certain shape—like a cube or pyramid. Crystals develop whenever a solid slowly forms from a liquid. A bag of sugar contains tiny sugar crystals. When you put sugar

crystals into hot water, the crystals *dissolve*, or break up into tiny pieces that you can't see. Sugar dissolved in water is called a sugar **solution**.

What You'll Need:

- 1 cup water
- measuring cup
- medium-size, microwave-safe bowl
- microwave oven
- oven mitts
- heat-resistant flat surface
- 1⅔ cups sugar
- mixing spoon
- aluminum pie pan
- scissors
- yarn

What to Do:

1. Put 1 cup water into a medium-size, microwave-safe bowl. Put the bowl into a microwave oven. Ask an adult to help you heat it on high power for 3 minutes.

2. Ask an adult to help you remove the bowl from the oven using the oven mitts. Put it on a heat-resistant flat surface.

3. Slowly add 1⅓ cups sugar to the hot water. Stir with a mixing spoon until all the sugar dissolves. This is your sugar solution.

4. Carefully pour the sugar solution into an aluminum pie pan.

5. With the scissors, cut a piece of yarn, about a foot long. Wet the yarn, and rub some dry sugar onto it.

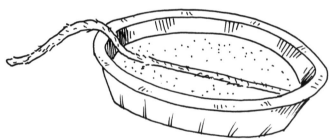

6. Hang one end of the yarn over the edge of the pie pan, and lay the rest of the yarn across the sugar solution. Allow the yarn to sink into the solution.

7. Put the aluminum pie pan in a sunny place where it won't be disturbed. Leave the sugar solution for 1 week, then lift the yarn out. What's attached to the yarn?

What Happened:

After a week, large crystals of sugar candy were attached to the yarn. The sugar candy formed for two reasons: boiling water can dissolve more sugar than cooler water, and a large amount of water can dissolve more sugar than a small amount of water. The hot sugar solution you made was **saturated**. It contained as much sugar as it could hold. When the solution was left in a sunny spot, the water cooled and **evaporated,** or escaped into the air. The solution could then no longer hold so much sugar. The sugar particles slowly came out of the solution, and joined the sugar crystals on the yarn. After a week, large crystals of sugar candy had formed. You can eat the candy.

One Step Further:

Ready to make a different kind of candy? Pour a package of flavored gelatin, like strawberry Jell-O, into a small bowl. With a medicine dropper, add a drop of cold water to the gelatin. Let the water seep in. Add a second drop of cold water to the same spot. Let the water seep in. Continue doing this until you've added 10 drops of water to the gelatin. With a fork, scoop up the jellied spot. You have a gumdrop. You can eat the gumdrop.

Questions:

1. Do you like candy? Why?

2. You prepared a sugar solution to make candy crystals. What do you think a salt solution is?

3. Gems—such as diamonds—are large, beautiful crystals. Can you name other gems that are crystals?

4. Scientists use X rays to determine the arrangement of atoms in a crystal. What else can X rays be used for? Can you name some other kinds of rays?

5. An element is made of only one kind of atom, and has certain properties. For example: the element iron, made of iron atoms, is a heavy metal that can conduct electricity; the element carbon, made of carbon atoms, can form long chains and balls. Pretend that you've created five new elements. What are their properties? What will you name them?

Cabbage Colors

Can cabbage juice be used to find out if household items are acids or bases?

Background:

Acids and bases are **chemicals** that have different **properties** or characteristics. A substance that changes color in the presence of an acid or base is called an **indicator**. Cabbage juice is an indicator. Acids make it turn pink; bases make it turn green or blue; and neutral substances, which are neither acids nor bases, cause no color change.

What You'll Need:

- half a red cabbage
- knife
- 4 cups water
- measuring cups
- large microwave-safe casserole with cover
- microwave oven
- oven mitts
- heat-resistant flat surface
- slotted spoon
- ladle
- nine clear, colorless plastic cups
- measuring spoons

- 1 teaspoon lemon juice
- 1 teaspoon salt
- 1 teaspoon baking soda
- 1 teaspoon vinegar
- 1 teaspoon orange juice
- 1 teaspoon sugar
- 1 teaspoon dishwashing liquid
- 1 teaspoon plain water
- 1 teaspoon window cleaner

What to Do:

1. Ask an adult to help you cut half a red cabbage into chunks.

2. Place 4 cups water into a large, microwave-safe casserole. Put the casserole into a microwave oven. Ask an adult to help you heat it on high power for 5 minutes.

3. With the help of an adult, use the oven mitts to remove the casserole from the oven and place it on a heat-resistant flat surface.

4. Carefully place the cabbage chunks into the hot water, cover the casserole, and leave it for 30 minutes.

5. With a slotted spoon, remove the cabbage chunks from the bowl and throw them away. The purple cabbage juice in the bowl is your indicator.

6. Ladle ¼ cup of indicator into each of nine clear, colorless plastic cups.

7. Add a teaspoon of the following substances, one to each cup: lemon juice, salt, baking soda, vinegar, orange juice, sugar, dishwashing liquid, plain water, window cleaner. Note any color change in the indicator.

8. Use the rest of the indicator to test substances of your choice.

What Happened:

Indicators change color because they combine with the different particles produced when acids and bases break up in water. Lemon juice, vinegar, and orange juice are acids. They made the cabbage juice turn pink. Baking soda, dishwashing liquid, and window cleaner are bases. They made the cabbage juice turn green or blue. Salt, sugar, and plain water are neutral. They caused no color change.

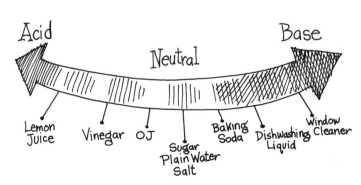

One Step Further:

Vinegar is also used in making curds and whey. Put ¼ cup whole milk into a small bowl. Add 2 tablespoons of white vinegar, and stir. Observe the mixture after 10 minutes. It contains solid lumps, called *curds,* and a watery liquid, called *whey*. What do you think happened?

Questions:

1. Can you name a food made with cabbage?

2. If you added grapefruit juice to the indicator, what do you think would happen? Why?

3. The word *cabbage* comes from the French word *caboche,* which means "big head." Why do you think cabbage was given this name?

4. Some strong acids, like sulfuric acid, can cause acid burns. How do you think people should handle sulfuric acid? What should a person do if he or she gets splashed with sulfuric acid?

5. People who have tropical fish use indicators to test the water in their tanks. Why do you think they do this? Can you think of some other uses for indicators?

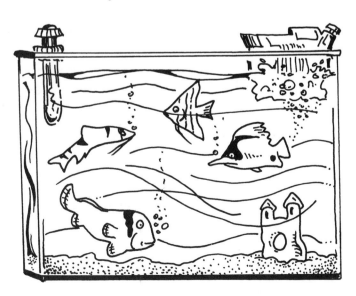

Invisible Ink

Can baking soda be used to make invisible ink?

Background:

Baking soda is a base. Purple grape juice is an **indicator**. An indicator changes color when it combines with a base. (See "Cabbage Colors.")

What You'll Need:

- two small plastic cups
- measuring spoons
- 1 tablespoon baking soda
- 1 tablespoon water
- spoon
- cotton-tipped swabs
- sheet of white paper
- ¼ cup purple grape juice

What to Do:

1. Put 1 tablespoon baking soda into a small plastic cup.

2. Add 1 tablespoon water, and mix with a spoon. This is your ink.

3. Wet a cotton-tipped swab with the ink. Use the swab to write your name on a sheet of white paper.

4. Let the paper dry. It will look blank.

5. Pour ¼ cup of purple grape juice into a separate plastic cup.

6. Dip a fresh cotton-tipped swab into the grape juice, and rub it over the name written in baking soda. What happens?

What Happened:

When you rubbed grape juice over the invisible name, the name appeared in grayish-green letters. This happened because the baking soda, or *base,* made the grape juice, or *indicator,* change color.

One Step Further:

When you're done with invisible ink, try your hand at making paint. Put ¼ cup blueberries and 1 tablespoon water into a bowl. With a spoon, mash the blueberries into the water, until the water turns reddish-purple. Use a cotton-tipped swab to make a picture with your paint.

Questions:

1. Grapes can be purple, green, or red. What other fruits come in more than one color?

2. Today, most dyes are made from chemicals. In the past, however, dyes were made from dandelion flowers, beets, grass, and other plants. What do you think plant dyes were used for?

3. How could you write a message *without* writing tools such as pens, pencils, crayons, markers, cotton-tipped swabs, or paintbrushes?

4. In science fiction stories, people sometimes drink chemical brews and become invisible. Do you think this is possible? Why?

5. Can you make up a code for writing secret messages?

Water Spout

Can you produce a water spout by combining an acid and a base?

Background:

Acids and bases are **chemicals** with different **properties**. When an acid combines with a base, they react with each other and change to form new products.

What You'll Need:

- 1 cup vinegar
- measuring cup
- empty plastic 1-liter soda bottle
- warm water
- large baking pan
- flat surface
- measuring spoon
- 2 tablespoons baking soda
- small plastic cup
- spoon

What to Do:

1. Put 1 cup vinegar into a plastic 1-liter soda bottle. Add warm water until the bottle is almost full.

2. Place the baking pan on a flat surface. Place the soda bottle upright in the middle of the baking pan.

3. Put 2 tablespoons baking soda into a small plastic cup. Add 2 tablespoons water. Mix with a spoon.

4. Quickly add the baking soda–water mixture to the soda bottle. What happens?

What Happened:

Vinegar contains an acid called *acetic* acid. Baking soda, also called *sodium bicarbonate,* is a base. When baking soda was added to the vinegar in the bottle, the acid and base reacted. They produced several products, including carbon dioxide and heat energy. The carbon dioxide gas quickly *expanded,* or spread out. It shot out of the bottle, carrying liquid with it. This produced a water spout.

One Step Further:

Pour a can of lemon-lime soda into a transparent plastic cup. Add a few raisins. After a few minutes, the raisins begin to move up and down in the soda. Why does this happen?

Questions:

1. Can you name some gases, other than carbon dioxide?

2. Does soda that has lost its gas bubbles taste good?

3. Can you name an animal that has a water spout?

4. Baking powder, which contains sodium bicarbonate as well as an acid, is used to make cakes rise. How do you think baking powder works?

5. Our bodies contain many acids. Amino acids make up **proteins** and nucleic acids. Nucleic acids make up DNA. Why do we need proteins and DNA?

Polish the Pennies

How do you make dull pennies shine?

Background:

Pennies are made of zinc, with a thin coating of copper. Copper metal is shiny, so new pennies gleam. Old pennies, however, become dull. This happens because copper combines with oxygen from the air to form copper oxide. Copper oxide makes pennies look drab and dirty.

What You'll Need:

- ¼ cup white vinegar
- measuring cup
- shallow plastic bowl
- 1 teaspoon salt
- measuring spoon
- spoon
- five dull pennies
- water
- paper towels

What to Do:

1. Put ¼ cup white vinegar into a shallow plastic bowl.

2. Add 1 teaspoon salt, and stir with a spoon.

3. Drop five dull pennies into the bowl, and leave them for 30 seconds.

4. Remove the pennies from the bowl, rinse them with water, and lay them on a paper towel to dry. How do they look?

What Happened:

The pennies look shiny. This happens because copper oxide *dissolves,* or breaks up, in a mixture of salt and a weak acid, like vinegar. When the copper oxide is dissolved, the pennies gleam.

One Step Further:

Use some more pennies to put copper plating on a screw. Put ¼ cup vinegar and 1 teaspoon salt into a plastic bowl. Mix them together. Put 25 dull pennies into the bowl, and leave them for 10 minutes. Remove the pennies. Put a clean screw into the bowl. Do not use a screw that is already copper or brass. Remove the screw after 30 minutes. How does the screw look?

Questions:

1. Can you name some metals, other than zinc, copper, and brass?

2. What are some metal things in your home?

3. Do you think your pennies would get clean if you substituted another acid, like lemon juice, for vinegar?

4. When metals are exposed to air, water, and other substances, they may *corrode*—change color and wear away. Can you give some examples of corroded metal objects?

5. Acid rain sometimes forms when air pollutants combine with water droplets in the air. Do you think acid rain is good or bad? Why?

Fresh Fruit

Adult Help Required

How do you stop cut fruit from turning brown?

Background:

Certain fruits, like apples and bananas, turn brown when they're cut. This happens because some of the cells that make up the fruits become damaged. The torn cells release chemicals that *react,* or combine, with oxygen from the air. This makes the cut part of the fruit turn brown.

What You'll Need:

- two plates
- flat surface
- ¼ cup lemon juice
- measuring cup
- small, shallow bowl
- knife
- banana
- apple

What to Do:

1. Place two plates on a flat surface.

2. Pour ¼ cup lemon juice into a small, shallow bowl.

3. Ask an adult to help you cut two slices of banana and two slices of apple.

4. Put one piece of apple and one piece of banana on the first plate.

5. Dip the other piece of apple and the other piece of banana into the lemon juice. Put them on the second plate.

6. Wait for one hour and look at the fruits. What happened?

What Happened:

The undipped fruit slices turned brown, and the dipped fruit slices kept their original color. This happened because the lemon juice contains ascorbic acid. Ascorbic acid keeps the chemicals in the fruits from combining with oxygen. This stops the fruits from turning brown.

One Step Further:

Use the refrigerator and some more fruit to try another experiment. Ask an adult to help you cut two slices of apple and two slices of banana. Put a piece of apple and a piece of banana on each of two plates. Put the first plate in the refrigerator, and leave the second plate at room temperature. Check the fruits after one hour. What happened?

Questions:

1. If you bit an apple or banana instead of cutting it, do you think it would still turn brown?

2. What kinds of fruits would you use to make a fruit salad? How would you keep the fruit salad looking fresh?

3. Ascorbic acid is also called vitamin C. Can you name some other vitamins? Why do people need vitamins?

4. Bananas range in length from around 4 to 12 inches. How many 4-inch bananas would have to be stacked up to be about as tall as you? How many 12-inch bananas?

5. Earth is the only planet in the solar system with a large amount of oxygen in its atmosphere. Why do you think this is?

Plump Potato, Thin Potato

How can we make potato cells gain or lose water?

Background:

When solids *dissolve,* or break up, in liquids, they form **solutions**. A cup of coffee, for example, contains a solution of coffee particles in water. The cells that make up living things also contain solutions. Potato cells, for example, contain solutions of starch and **protein** in water. Potato cells have tiny openings in their *cell membranes,* or skins. Water can pass through these openings. This process is called *osmosis.*

What You'll Need:

- knife
- raw potato
- 1 cup water
- measuring cup
- two clear, transparent plastic cups

- ⅛ cup salt
- spoon
- flat surface
- ruler

What to Do:

1. Ask an adult to help you cut two raw potato cubes, each about 1 inch across. The potato cubes should be equal in size, and should not have any peel on them.

2. Pour 1 cup water into each of 2 plastic cups.

3. Leave the first cup as is. Put ⅛ cup salt into the second cup, and stir with a spoon. Place the cups on a flat surface.

4. Place one potato cube into each cup. Leave the potato cubes in the cups for 6 hours, then take them out and measure them. Has their size changed?

What Happened:

The potato cube in the plain water *swelled,* or got larger, and the potato cube in the salt water *shrank,* or got smaller. This happened because of osmosis. During osmosis, water moves from a solution that has fewer solid particles to a solution that has more solid particles. In the first cup, the plain water had fewer solid particles than the potato cells. Therefore, water moved into the potato cells, and the potato cube swelled. In the second cup, the potato cells had fewer solid particles than the salt solution. Therefore, water moved out of the potato cells, and the potato cube shrank.

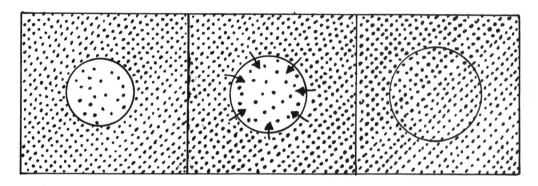

One Step Further:

Pour 1 cup water into a plastic cup. Add several raisins to the cup, and leave them for 3 hours. What happens to the raisins?

Questions:

1. Cooks sometimes soak raisins before using them to make cakes and candies. Why do you think they do this?

2. Soft drinks, like sodas, are solutions. What do you think they contain?

3. Do you think osmosis is occurring when the roots of plants take up water from the soil?

4. There are many ways to cook and prepare potatoes. Can you name some? What kinds of potatoes do you like best?

5. Years ago, people covered fish and meat with salt to keep them from spoiling. Why do you think this worked?

Pickle Plant

How do you make quick pickles?

Adult Help Required

Background:

Foods spoil when harmful **microbes**—tiny life-forms such as bacteria and fungi—grow on them. To keep unwanted microbes from growing, foods are preserved. Methods of preservation include canning, freezing, drying, treating with radiation, and pickling. People have been pickling foods for thousands of years.

What You'll Need:

- large cucumber
- water
- knife
- deep bowl
- flat surface
- 1 tablespoon salt
- measuring spoon

- spoon
- small plate
- heavy object (like a large can of vegetables)
- 1 tablespoon sugar
- ½ cup white vinegar
- plastic wrap
- chopped dill (optional)

What to Do:

1. Thoroughly wash a large cucumber with water.

2. Ask an adult to cut the cucumber into very thin slices.

3. Place a deep bowl on a flat surface. Put the cucumber slices into the bowl. Add 1 tablespoon salt, and mix with a spoon.

4. Put a small plate on top of the slices. The plate should be faceup so its bottom is pressing against the slices. Place something heavy on the plate, like a large can of vegetables, so the plate presses even harder.

5. Leave the cucumber slices at room temperature for 1 hour. Drain off the liquid.

6. Mix 1 tablespoon sugar with ½ cup white vinegar. Pour the mixture over the cucumber slices. Mix with a spoon.

7. Cover the bowl containing the cucumber slices with plastic wrap. Put the bowl into the refrigerator for 3 hours.

8. Remove the bowl from the refrigerator, and drain the liquid. You now have crispy pickle slices. Sprinkle with chopped dill if you like. You can eat the pickle slices.

What Happened:

You turned cucumber slices into pickle slices in two steps. First, you used salt to *dehydrate,* or remove water from, the cucumber slices. This process, called *osmosis,* made the cucumber slices crunchy. (See "Plump Potato, Thin Potato.") Second, you used sugar and vinegar to *ferment,* or make chemical changes in, the cucumbers. This gave the slices a "pickle" flavor. **Dehydration** and fermentation preserve foods by stopping the growth of harmful bacteria.

One Step Further:

When bacteria grow in clear broth, they make it look cloudy. *Preservatives* keep bacteria from growing. To see which preservative works best, open a can of clear chicken broth. Put ¼ cup broth into each of three clear, transparent plastic cups. Stir 1 teaspoon salt into the first cup. Stir 1 teaspoon white vinegar into the second cup. Leave the third cup as is. Place the three cups in a warm place for 24 hours, then look at them. Which is the clearest? Which is the cloudiest?

Questions:

1. What kinds of foods go well with pickles?

2. Some microbes cause diseases in people. Can you name some of these diseases?

3. Many foods, in addition to cucumbers, can be pickled. Which foods do you think would taste best pickled?

4. Some microbes break down dead plants and animals. Why is this important for the environment?

5. Pretend you're on a camping trip, and you have no refrigerator, freezer, cooler, salt, or vinegar. How could you preserve food, like meat, vegetables, and fruits?

Mottled Milk

What happens when spots of food coloring are added to milk?

Background:

Liquids, such as milk and food coloring, are made of tiny particles called **molecules**. The molecules of a liquid are always bouncing around and bumping into each other.

What You'll Need:

- aluminum pie pan
- flat surface
- ½ cup milk
- measuring cup
- toothpicks
- red, yellow, and blue food coloring

What to Do:

1. Put the aluminum pie pan on a flat surface.

2. Pour ½ cup milk into the pie pan.

3. Dip a toothpick into a bottle of red food coloring. Lightly touch the toothpick to the milk. Do this in several places.

4. Repeat step 3 with the other shades of food coloring, so that the milk is *mottled,* or dotted with colors.

5. Leave the pie pan undisturbed for 10 minutes, then observe the contents. What happened?

What Happened:

The food coloring spread out and swirled through the milk. When the food coloring was added to the milk, the molecules of food coloring bounced around and spread out. This is called **diffusion**. During diffusion, molecules move from a place where they are crowded together to a place where they are less crowded. Because of diffusion, the molecules of food coloring moved from the spots you made to the rest of the milk. If left alone, the food coloring and milk would eventually mix together to form one color.

One Step Further:

Make some pretty paper. Dip several small sheets of white paper into the colorful milk, one at a time. Lay the sheets on newspaper, and let them dry. What color are they?

Questions:

1. Why is milk good for you?

2. What do people use food coloring for? Give some examples.

3. Do you think food coloring would diffuse through water?

4. In addition to diffusing through liquids, molecules can diffuse through gases, like air. Can you give an example of diffusion in air?

5. Can you write a short poem using some of the following words? Milk, silk, bounce, pounce, bump, jump, swirl, twirl, spot, dot.

Capsized Cup

Can air pressure hold water in a capsized, or overturned, cup?

Background:

There is a layer of air, hundreds of miles thick, that covers our planet. This is called **Earth's atmosphere**. The air is made of small particles called **molecules**. Air molecules bounce around—up, down, and sideways—pushing on everything they touch. The "pushing force" of the air molecules is called **air pressure**.

What You'll Need:

- small plastic cup
- water
- 3-by-5-inch index card
- sink

What to Do:

1. Fill a small plastic cup with water.

2. Put a 3-by-5-inch index card over the top of the cup, and hold it in place with your hand. The card must cover the entire opening of the cup.

3. Turn the cup upside down over the sink, and let go of the index card. Does the water flow out?

What Happened:

The water didn't flow out. Air pressure pushing up on the index card held it in place. The card blocked the cup's opening, so the water couldn't stream out.

One Step Further:

Can you stop water from flowing out of a holey container? Get an empty plastic container with a tight-fitting lid, like a small margarine container. Ask an adult to make a hole in the bottom of the container and a hole in the lid. (A nail can be used to make the holes.) Hold the container over the sink, fill it with water, and put on the lid. Does the water flow out? Repeat the experiment, but this time, quickly put your finger over the hole in the lid. What happens now?

Questions:

1. What do you think water pressure is?

2. When are you likely to notice air pressure pushing on your body?

3. A dam is a barrier that holds back water. Why do you think people sometimes build dams across rivers?

4. Do you think the capsized cup experiment would work on the Moon? Why?

5. In addition to thinking about air pressure, scientists on space shuttles often perform experiments—such as growing plants or making crystals—to see what happens in an environment without **gravity,** which is a force that pulls everything toward Earth. If you were a scientist, what would you make or grow in outer space? Why?

Taste Test

If you close your eyes and hold your nose, can you tell what you're eating?

Background:

Smell is an important part of taste. When we eat something, our tongue sends a "taste message" to our brain, and our nose sends a "smell message" to our brain. Our brain puts together the taste and smell messages and determines the food's flavor.

What You'll Need:

- raw potato
- apple
- knife
- flat surface
- regular potato chip
- barbecue flavor potato chip
- vanilla wafer
- chocolate wafer
- white bread
- whole wheat bread
- strawberry yogurt
- blueberry yogurt
- spoons
- plastic cup
- water

What to Do:

1. Ask an adult to cut a thin slice of raw potato, without the peel, and a thin slice of apple, without the peel.

2. Line up the following items on a flat surface: the slice of raw potato, the slice of apple, a regular potato chip, a barbecue flavor potato chip, a vanilla wafer, a chocolate wafer, a slice of white bread, a slice of whole wheat bread, a spoonful of strawberry yogurt, and a spoonful of blueberry yogurt.

3. Fill a plastic cup with drinking water. Then close your eyes and hold your nose.

4. Ask an adult to hand you an item to taste. Try to identify it.

5. Take a sip of water to clear your mouth.

6. Ask the adult to hand you another item to taste. Try to identify it.

7. Repeat steps 5 and 6 until you've tasted all the items. Ask the adult how many you got right.

What Happened:

You probably had a hard time telling the difference between foods that have *similar textures,* or feel alike—like the potato and apple, the regular and barbecue flavor potato chips, and so on. This happened because your brain didn't get information about how the food smelled. Without this information, your brain wasn't able to detect the food's flavor.

One Step Further:

Test your taste buds. Pour a little grape juice into a cup. Dip a toothpick into the juice, and touch the toothpick to the back of your tongue. Dip the toothpick again, and touch it to the side of your tongue. Dip the toothpick once more, and touch it to the front of your tongue. Where does the juice taste sweetest?

Questions:

1. When we have a stuffy nose, food tastes funny. Why do you think this is?

2. When cave dwellers lived, there were no farms or stores. What do you think they ate? Did their food taste the same as ours?

3. Can you name some pairs of foods that have similar textures, other than those mentioned above?

4. What are your favorite foods? Do you think everyone has the same favorite foods? Why?

5. Great chefs say meals should taste good *and* look good, with pretty colors. What foods would you include in a delicious, beautiful meal?

Straw Sounds

Can reeds be made from a drinking straw?

Background:

Oboes and bassoons are musical instruments that use *reeds,* which are thin strips made from the stems of giant grass plants. When a musician blows air into the mouthpiece of an instrument, the reeds *vibrate,* or shake back and forth rapidly. The vibrating reeds make the air inside the instrument vibrate. This produces sound waves. The sound waves travel to the ears of a listener, who hears the instrument's tones.

What You'll Need:

- plastic drinking straw
- scissors

What to Do:

1. Flatten the end of a plastic drinking straw by squeezing it between your fingers.

2. With the scissors, cut off the corners of the straw's flat end, to make arrowlike points.

3. Hold the cut end of the straw lightly between your lips and blow gently. What kind of sound do you hear?

4. With the scissors, cut pieces off the bottom of the straw as you blow. What happens to the sound?

What Happened:

The pointed ends of the straw acted like reeds. When you blew air through the reeds, they vibrated. The vibrating reeds made the air in the straw vibrate. This produced a whistling sound. When the straw was cut, the whistling sound became higher. This happened because the sound waves got shorter. Short sound waves produce higher tones, and long sound waves produce lower tones.

One Step Further:

Try to make pepper jump. Cover the top of a plastic cup with a paper towel. Fasten the paper towel onto the cup with a rubber band. Place the cup on a flat surface, and sprinkle some pepper onto the paper towel. Put your mouth next to the cup. Now sing a musical scale, from high notes to low notes. Sing loudly. What does the pepper do?

Questions:

1. What musical instruments, other than oboes and bassoons, do people blow into?

2. Do you *reed* a book, *rede* a book, or *read* a book?

3. What is a song? Which songs do you like best?

4. To play a guitar, a musician strums its strings. How do vibrating guitar strings make sounds? What are some other stringed instruments?

5. What are some plant parts, besides stems? What do people use plant parts for?

Egg Stand

Can salt particles hold up an egg?

Background:

Buildings and bridges must resist **gravity,** a force that pulls everything toward Earth. They must also withstand other forces, like wind, that push against them. *Trusses,* or outside beams, help buildings and bridges remain upright.

Trusses can also be found on other structures. For example, the giant ball at the entrance to Disney World's Epcot Center is held up by beams that act as trusses around its base.

What You'll Need:

- 1 tablespoon salt
- measuring spoon
- flat surface
- cooled hard-boiled egg

What to Do:

1. Put 1 tablespoon salt on a flat surface.

2. Place a cooled hard-boiled egg in the salt, so that the egg stands up.

3. Gently blow away the salt. Does the egg remain standing? Why?

What Happened:

The egg remained standing because it was held up by just a few grains of salt around its base. These salt particles functioned as *trusses,* or support structures, to hold up the egg.

One Step Further:

How strong are eggshells? Get the shells from two cracked eggs. Wash them, and let them dry. Trim the bases of the eggshells with nail scissors, to make four "domes" of about equal size. Arrange the eggshell domes in a square, 9 inches across. Place a thin book on the eggshell square. Do the shells crack? Keep adding thin books until the shells crack.

Questions:

1. What's the tallest building you ever saw? What city was it in?

2. Which parts of our bodies help us stand up straight?

3. What kinds of things might be used to construct a house or building?

4. How many eggs are in a carton that holds 1 dozen eggs? 1½ dozen eggs? 2 dozen eggs?

5. If you could live anywhere you wanted, where would your house be? What would it look like? On a separate piece of paper, draw a picture of your ideal home.

How do you make a thaumatrope?

Background:

When we look at something, our eyes "hold" the picture for a fraction of a second after we've seen it. That's why movies seem to move. A movie is made of a series of photographs. The photographs are projected on a screen, one after another, very quickly. Because our eyes still see an earlier picture when a new one appears, the pictures blend together. This makes the images seem to move. *Thaumatropes* are moving-picture toys, invented in the 1800s.

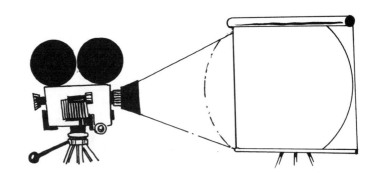

What You'll Need:

- scissors
- white paper
- markers
- drinking straw
- transparent tape

What to Do:

1. With the scissors, cut two equal-sized squares of white paper, about 3 inches across.

2. Use markers to draw cookies on one piece of paper, and an empty cookie jar on the other piece of paper.

3. Attach a plastic straw to the back of one of the drawings with transparent tape.

4. Tape the two drawings together, back to back. This is your thaumatrope.

5. Spin the thaumatrope by quickly rolling the straw back and forth between your hands. Do you see the cookies inside the jar?

What Happened:

Your brain held each image—the cookies and the cookie jar—for a moment after you'd seen it. As you flipped the pictures back and forth, the cookies and the cookie jar blended together. This made it look like the cookies were in the jar.

One Step Further:

Look at both groups of cookies. Which center cookie is larger, the left one or the right one?

Questions:

1. What kinds of devices are used to take photographs?

2. Can you think of some pictures, other than cookies and a cookie jar, that would make good thaumatropes?

3. Children today have some toys that were not known in the 1800s. Can you name some of these modern toys?

4. Pretend you're making a movie about your favorite storybook character—such as Madeline, Babar, or any character you like. You plan to let your friends play the parts. Which friend would play which part? Why?

5. People sometimes "see things" that aren't there. For example, thirsty people in the desert may think they see water. Can you think of other situations where people might "see things"?

Butter Beater

How long does it take to make butter?

Background:

Butter is a yellow spread made from cow's milk. To make butter, the *cream*, or fatty part of the milk, is separated from the rest of the milk. The cream is then *churned*, or beaten, to make butter.

What You'll Need:

- ½ pint whipping cream
- glass jar with lid
- nickel
- dishwashing liquid
- water
- strainer
- coffee filter
- small, deep bowl
- spoon

What to Do:

1. Pour ½ pint whipping cream into a glass jar. The jar shouldn't be more than half full.

2. Carefully wash a nickel with dishwashing liquid and warm water. Drop the nickel into the jar, and tighten the lid.

3. Shake the jar for about 15 minutes. If you get tired of shaking, ask someone to help you.

4. After about 15 minutes, the cream will separate into a whitish liquid and a yellow solid. Pour off the liquid.

5. Line a small strainer with a coffee filter, and place the strainer over a small, deep bowl.

6. Spoon the yellow solid into the coffee filter, and press down with the spoon—to squeeze more water out. The yellow solid remaining in the coffee filter is butter. You can eat the butter.

What Happened:

Whipping cream is a mixture of tiny blobs of fat floating in water. The blobs of fat are surrounded by thin *membranes,* or skins. When you shook the cream with the nickel, the nickel broke up the membranes of the fat blobs. The fat blobs then joined together to make butter.

One Step Further:

Now try making cheese from yogurt. Get an 8-ounce container of strawberry yogurt. Check the ingredients to make sure the yogurt doesn't contain gelatin. Line a small strainer with a coffee filter, and place the strainer over a small, deep bowl. Spoon the strawberry yogurt into the coffee filter. Lightly cover the strainer and bowl with plastic wrap, and place them in the refrigerator. The liquid will drain out of the yogurt. After 36 hours, the coffee filter will contain soft, strawberry-flavored cheese. You can eat the cheese.

Questions:

1. In old-fashioned butter churns, cream is whipped with a wooden paddle. What do you think the paddle does?

2. Can you name some foods that are made with butter? with milk? with cheese?

3. What is a dairy farm? Can you name some other kinds of farms?

4. Milk is produced by mammals. What are some features of mammals? Can you name a mammal that lives in the ocean? that lives on land? that flies?

5. Milk from many animals—such as cows, sheep, goats, buffalo, and camels—can be used to make cheese. Pretend that you have been asked to invent a new type of cheese. What kind of milk would you use? How would you flavor the cheese? What would you call it?

Fruit Frosty

How do you make a frosty fruit treat?

Background:

Heat is a form of energy that can *flow,* or move, from warmer areas to colder areas. In a glass of ice water, for example, heat flows from the water to the ice. The water becomes colder, and the ice melts. Melting ice absorbs a lot of heat, so the water eventually becomes very cold.

What You'll Need:

- ¼ cup grape juice
- ¼ cup apple juice
- measuring cup
- small glass jar
- spoon
- medium-size mixing bowl
- 6 cups ice
- ½ cup rock salt
- two dish towels

What to Do:

1. Put ¼ cup grape juice and ¼ cup apple juice into a small glass jar. Mix them with a spoon.

2. Place the jar into a medium-size mixing bowl, and surround the jar with ice.

3. Sprinkle ½ cup rock salt in and around the ice.

4. Fold two dish towels in half, lengthwise, and wrap them around the bowl.

5. Leave the bowl for 2 hours. An apple-grape frosty forms in the jar. You can eat the frosty.

What Happened:

Salt lowers the melting point of ice, which makes the ice melt more quickly than usual. In this experiment, the apple-grape juice was surrounded by a large quantity of melting ice. The melting ice absorbed heat from the juice, which became colder and colder. Eventually, the juice formed a frozen treat.

One Step Further:

How do you attach ice to a string? Get a piece of thread, about 9 inches long. Float an ice cube in a cup of water. Lay one end of the thread over the surface of the ice cube. With a salt shaker, sprinkle two shakes of salt on and around the thread. Wait for one minute. Lift the thread by the free end. Does it pick up the ice cube?

Questions:

1. Why does a person feel chilly when he or she is outside on a cold day?

2. Why do people sprinkle salt on icy roads?

3. Can you name some things that flow, besides heat?

4. Where does most of the heat on the Earth's surface come from? Why is outer space much colder than Earth?

5. Scientific laws say that heat flows from warm to cold places; time moves forward (you can't go back in time); objects fall down (not up); and things tend to get disorganized (for example, your room gets messy if no one cleans it). If you could change one of these laws, which would you change? Why?

Ice Lift

What happens when water is placed in the freezer?

Background:

Everything in the world, from the tiniest grain of salt to the largest ocean, is made of **matter**. Matter comes in three forms—solid, liquid, and gas—and can change from one form to another. For example, liquid water can freeze to form solid ice, and solid ice can melt to form liquid water.

What You'll Need:

- small plastic cup
- water
- small square of cardboard
- freezer

What to Do:

1. Fill a small plastic cup to the rim with water.

2. Put a square of cardboard over the top of the cup.

3. Place the cup, with the cardboard in place, in the freezer. Leave the cup for 24 hours, then look at it. What happened?

What Happened:

The water in the cup froze and formed ice. The ice pushed out of the cup and lifted the cardboard. In nature, most things *contract*, or take up less space, when they freeze. Water, however, *expands*, or takes up more space, when it freezes. That's why the ice rose above the surface of the cup.

One Step Further:

Try freezing a balloon. Blow up a small balloon, and tie off the end. With a tape measure, measure how large around the balloon is. Put the balloon in the freezer, and leave it for 2 hours. Take the balloon out, and quickly measure it again. What happened?

Questions:

1. Can you name some things, found in the kitchen, that are made of matter?

2. What would happen if a sealed glass bottle, full of water, was placed in the freezer?

3. When water boils, it changes form and becomes steam. What is steam?

4. Where is most of the ice on Earth found? What are some things people use ice for?

5. Scientists believe there may be ice on the Moon. How could this help humans live there? Would you like to live on the Moon?

Water Works

How do you desalinate water?

! Adult Help Required

Background:

Arid, or dry, parts of the world have little groundwater, and few lakes, rivers, and streams. Because of this, they lack fresh water. To get usable water, dry areas must remove salt from seawater. This is called *desalination.* Desalination produces salt-free water for drinking and cooking.

What You'll Need:

- 2 cups water
- measuring cup
- large bowl
- 3 teaspoons salt
- measuring spoon
- spoon
- small glass
- plastic wrap
- marble

What to Do:

1. Pour 2 cups water into a large bowl. Add 3 teaspoons salt. Stir with a spoon until the salt *dissolves,* or breaks up into tiny pieces you can't see. Taste a drop of the water to see how salty it is.

2. Place a small glass in the center of the bowl.

3. Cover the bowl with plastic wrap. Place a marble in the middle of the plastic wrap, centered over the cup. The plastic wrap should be slightly lower in the center.

4. Put the wrapped bowl, with the marble in place, in a sunny spot for several hours. Water will collect in the cup.

5. Remove the plastic wrap and taste the water in the cup. Is it salty?

What Happened:

The glass contained *desalinated,* or salt-free, water. The sun heated the water in the bowl. The warm water **evaporated,** or escaped from the bowl, to form water vapor gas. The salt, however, was too heavy to evaporate. The water vapor particles *condensed,* or came together, to form water drops on the bottom of the plastic wrap. Because the plastic wrap was lower in the center, the water drops rolled to the middle, and dripped into the glass. The glass, therefore, contained desalinated water.

One Step Further:

Get a close-up look at **condensation**. Find two small glass jars with lids. Pour ½ cup water into each jar. Leave the lids off. Ask an adult to help you microwave the jars on high power for 2 minutes, and then ask the adult to help remove the jars from the microwave using oven mitts. Put the jars on a heat-resistant flat surface. Turn the jar lids upside down, and place them over the tops of the jars. Fill the lid of the first jar with ice cubes. Leave the lid of the second jar as is. Observe the jars for a few minutes. Which lid begins to drip water first? Why?

Questions:

1. What's the difference between fresh water and seawater?

2. What are some things people use water for, other than cooking and drinking?

3. Countries that desalinate seawater include Israel and Kuwait. Look at a map or globe. What are some countries around Israel? around Kuwait?

4. Farmers in arid areas sometimes irrigate their crops. What do you think irrigation is?

5. Sometimes, areas that usually get enough rain have a *drought,* or very long dry spell. What do you think happens when there's a drought? What are some ways to conserve water during a drought?

All Fall Down

Can you change the center of gravity of a straw?

Background:

Gravity is a force that pulls all objects toward Earth. If you push an object over the edge of a table, it falls to the floor because of gravity. Gravity pulls most strongly on the part of an object where its weight seems to be concentrated. This spot is called the *center of gravity*. If an object is the same on both sides—like a baseball—the center of gravity is in the middle. If an object is not the same on both sides—like a baseball bat—the center of gravity is closer to the heavier part.

What You'll Need:

- five plastic straws, all the same size
- white glue
- 10 pieces of uncooked elbow macaroni
- table

What to Do:

1. Line up five straws, all the same size.

2. With white glue, paste the elbow macaroni to the straws as follows: four pieces near the end of the first straw, three pieces near the end of the second straw, two pieces near the end of the third straw, and one piece near the end of the fourth straw. Leave the last straw as is. Let the glue dry for at least 1 hour.

3. Lay the five straws on a table, with the plain ends at the table's edge. The macaroni should be touching the table.

4. Push the first straw over the edge of the table until it's just about to fall off. Don't let it fall. Leave it in place. The point on the straw where it just balances on the edge of the table is its center of gravity.

5. Repeat step 4 with each of the other straws.

6. Compare the centers of gravity of the straws.
   How do they differ?

What Happened:

The plain straw was the same on both ends, so
its center of gravity was in the middle. The straw with one piece of macaroni was
heavier on one end, so its center of gravity was a little closer to that end. As more
and more macaroni was added to a straw, the end became heavier and heavier. The
center of gravity, therefore, moved closer and closer to the end with the macaroni.

One Step Further:

Can you bend and balance? Stand with your
back against a wall, so that the back of your
feet touch the wall. Ask someone to put an
apple on the floor, right in front of you. Try to
bend over and pick up the apple *without
moving your feet.* Can you do it?

Questions:

1. Do you think the center of gravity of a baseball glove would be in the exact center?

2. If a straw had a piece of macaroni on each end, where would its center of
   gravity be?

3. How many words can you make up using the letters in "center of gravity"?

4. If you drew a line down the middle of a Pop-Tart, the two sides would look the
   same. Can you name some other things that look the same on both sides? If you
   look down at a paper plate, it looks the same on both sides, and all around. Can
   you name some other things that look the same all around?

5. Imagine that hurricane winds blow past two 500-foot towers—one shaped like a
   pyramid, and one shaped like a pole. Which tower is more likely to fall over?
   Why do you think so?

Balance Beam

Can a dipped fingertip push down a glass of water?

Background:

When you place a slice of lemon into a glass of water, some water is *displaced*, or pushed aside, to make room for the lemon slice. The displaced water has to go someplace, so the level of water in the glass rises.

What You'll Need:

- pencil with six flat sides (not a round pencil)
- flat surface
- 12-inch ruler
- water
- measuring cup
- two small plastic cups

What to Do:

1. Place a pencil with six flat sides on a flat surface.

2. Center a 12-inch ruler on the pencil. The 6-inch mark on the ruler should be directly over the middle of the pencil.

3. Pour ½ cup water into each of two small plastic cups.

4. Place a cup of water on each end of the ruler. Adjust the cups so that the ruler does not touch the table on either side. The ruler is then balanced.

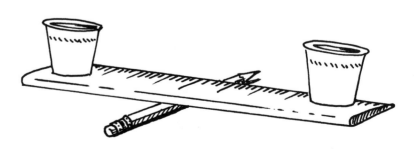

5. Carefully dip the tip of your finger into the water in one of the cups. Do not touch the edge of the cup. Does the ruler remain balanced?

What Happened:

The ruler did not remain balanced. The side you were touching moved down. Your fingertip displaced some water, which raised the level of water in the cup. This had the same effect as adding water to the cup, so the cup was pushed down.

One Step Further:

Watch the water level. Fill a small glass to the rim with water. Bend down, so that your eyes are even with the rim of the glass. Carefully drop raisins into the glass, one at a time. What happens to the surface of the water as the raisins are dropped in? How many raisins can you add without causing the water to overflow?

Questions:

1. Does the level of water in the bathtub rise when you get in to take a bath? Why?

2. One device used to weigh things is called a *balance*. Can you name another device used to weigh things?

3. In the balance beam experiment, how many inches of ruler are on either side of the pencil?

4. A shape with six equal sides is called a hexagon. What do we call a shape with three equal sides? four equal sides? five equal sides? What are some other shapes?

5. Pretend that you are outdoors and very thirsty. The only water available is in a well, but you can't reach the water, and you have no bucket. How could you use displacement to get some water?

Fat in Foods

How can you tell which foods contain fats?

Background:

People like foods that contain fats for several reasons. First, chemicals that give food their flavor and aroma *dissolve,* or break up, in fats. This makes food taste and smell good. Second, fats give food a creamy, smooth texture that people enjoy. Third, fatty foods make people feel full and satisfied. However, doctors advise people not to eat too many fatty foods, for health reasons.

What You'll Need:

- pretzel
- potato chip
- gumdrop
- slice of bread
- cookie
- lollipop
- small spoonfuls of peanut butter
- small spoonfuls of jelly
- small spoonfuls of mayonnaise
- small spoonfuls of margarine
- small pieces of chocolate
- small pieces of hot dog
- small pieces of cheese
- slice of apple
- slice of potato
- spoons
- knife
- large brown paper bag
- scissors
- pencil
- flat surface

What to Do:

1. Ask an adult to help you gather the foods listed above.

2. Cut open a large brown paper bag.

3. Lay the paper bag on a flat surface. With a pencil, draw one box for each food you're testing.

4. Write the name of a different test food at the bottom of each box.

5. Rub a bit of food into the correctly labeled box. Wet the dry foods with a little water, to help you rub them into the paper. Put the paper in a warm place and let it dry for 2 hours.

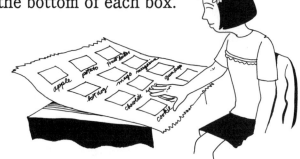

6. Hold the paper up to the light, and compare the stains left by the various foods. Fatty foods leave *translucent* stains, or stains that light can pass through. The bigger the stain, the fattier the food.

What Happened:

The paper *absorbed,* or took in, water and fat from the foods. As the paper dried, the water **evaporated,** or escaped into the air. The fats, however, remained on the paper, and left a stain. Unless you used "fat-free" varieties, the potato chip, cookie, peanut butter, mayonnaise, margarine, chocolate, hot dog, and cheese probably left fatty stains. The pretzel, gumdrop, bread, lollipop, jelly, apple, and potato probably didn't leave fatty stains.

One Step Further:

Cooking oil is a type of fat. Rub a few drops of cooking oil onto your hands. Hold your hands under cold running water. Does the oil wash off easily? Repeat the experiment, but this time rub a few drops of oil plus a few drops of dishwashing liquid onto your hands. Does the oil wash off easily this time?

Questions:

1. Do you sometimes eat foods that contain fats? If so, what kind?

2. How many words can you think of that rhyme with *fat*? Write them down on a separate piece of paper.

3. A good diet includes **proteins,** starches, and other things. What are some foods that contain proteins? starches?

4. Eskimos use a type of animal fat called *blubber.* Can you name some animals that have blubber? What do you think blubber is used for?

5. Though we shouldn't eat too many fatty foods, our bodies need some fats. What do you think our bodies use fats for?

Spin and Twirl

Can centrifugal force keep a grape from falling down?

Background:

When children spin around on a merry-go-round, they would fly off if they didn't hold on tight. In fact, all objects spinning around in a circle push out, away from the center of the circle. This happens because of centrifugal force.

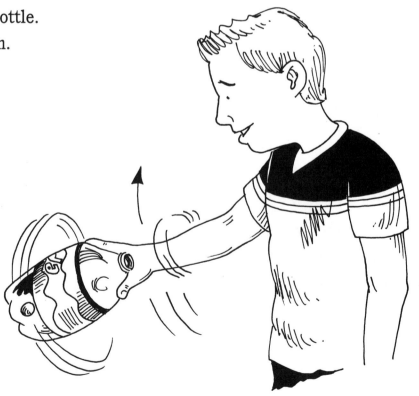

What You'll Need:

- round red grape
- empty plastic 2-liter soda bottle

What to Do:

1. Drop a round red grape into an empty plastic 2-liter soda bottle. Turn the bottle upside down. Does the grape fall out?

2. Drop the grape into the bottle again. This time, twirl the bottle, so that the grape whirls around the inside.

3. Keep twirling the bottle while slowly turning it upside down. Does the whirling grape fall out?

4. Continue holding the bottle upside down, and stop twirling it. What happens now?

What Happened:

The motionless grape fell out of the overturned bottle, because Earth's **gravity** pulled it down. The whirling grape, however, stayed inside the overturned bottle. This happened because centrifugal force made the whirling grape push out, against the inside of the bottle. This outward force was stronger than the downward pull of gravity. When the bottle stopped twirling, there was no more centrifugal force, and the grape fell out.

We use the term *centrifugal force* to help us understand how things move. However, centrifugal force is not a real force. It is actually **centripetal force** and **inertia** acting together. Centripetal force causes the grape to travel in a circle, and inertia makes the grape keep moving once it has started.

One Step Further:

Cut a strip, about 2 inches wide, off the long side of a piece of construction paper. Fold the strip in half and fashion it into a ring. Tape the ring shut. Place the ring on a flat surface, and put a round red grape inside. Twirl the ring, so the grape whirls around. While the grape is whirling, lift the ring. Does the grape keep moving in a circle?

Questions:

1. When would a child on a bicycle experience centrifugal force?

2. A carousel is a type of merry-go-round. How would you describe a carousel? Where would you find one?

3. Why did the grape in the twirling soda bottle move in a circle? Can you think of a situation where a grape in a twirling bottle wouldn't move in a circle?

4. Can you describe two ways in which gravity differs from centrifugal force?

5. Sir Isaac Newton and Albert Einstein were scientists who described gravity and other forces. Can you name some other scientists who did important work? If you became a scientist, what kind of work would you do?

Fluttering Fliers

How does an airplane fly?

Background:

In 1738, a Swiss scientist named Daniel Bernoulli made an important discovery. He found that fast-moving air has less pressure, or "pushing power," than slow-moving or still air. This is called **Bernoulli's principle**. Airplanes use this principle to fly.

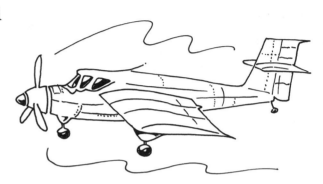

What You'll Need:

- scissors
- paper towel
- ruler

What to Do:

1. Cut a strip of paper towel, 2 inches wide and 8 inches long.

2. Hold the strip of paper towel flat in front of you, with the short end near your mouth, almost touching your lower lip. The paper will hang down.

3. Take a deep breath, then blow steadily over the top of the paper strip. What happens? Blow harder. What happens now?

What Happened:

When you blew over the paper strip, you made the air above the paper strip move fast. The air below the paper strip remained still. The still air under the paper strip had more pressure than the fast air above the paper strip. Therefore, the paper strip was pushed up. Airplanes use this effect to fly. As a plane races down the runway, the shape of the wings makes air flow faster over the wings than under the wings. This provides upward pressure, or "lift," to make the airplane take off and fly.

One Step Further:

Blow up two balloons and tie off the ends. Attach each balloon to a piece of string. Hang the balloons about 6 inches apart, or ask someone to hold them up for you. Using a straw, blow a stream of air between the balloons. The balloons will move together. Why does this happen?

Questions:

1. Can you name three things, besides flying, that we use air for?

2. Does a bird use Bernoulli's principle to fly?

3. Does a helium balloon use Bernoulli's principle to fly?

4. What country do you think a Swiss scientist comes from?

5. What are the names of the two American brothers who built and flew the first airplane? Do you think their airplane used Bernoulli's principle to fly?

Answers

Pages 8–9

OSF: The tiny pinhole in a plastic bag leaks for a moment. Then the polymers shrink, the hole seals, and the bag stops leaking.

1. Answers will vary. Sample answers: sunglasses, telephones, computer casings, cups, plates, disposable diapers, 3-ring binders, markers, pens, and furniture.
2. Answers will vary. Sample answers: rubber trees and other plants (like milkweed and mulberry). Things made of rubber include tires, rubber bands, galoshes, gloves, and balls.
3. When materials are recycled, they are treated and used again. Other materials can be recycled, including glass, paper, and aluminum cans.
4. To calculate the answer, subtract 1953 from the current year.
5. Answers will vary.

Pages 10–11

OSF: The peas *expand,* or enlarge, when they absorb water; and *shrink,* or get smaller, when the water evaporates.

1. The sculptures would dry out faster in a hot place, because water evaporates more quickly when it warms up.
2. Wheat flour is made from wheat. It's made in a mill, by grinding wheat grains into a powder.
3. Clay used by pottery makers is a type of soil, found in the ground.
4. Mixing the batter causes the protein gluten to form. Too much gluten makes the cake tough and chewy.
5. People allergic to wheat shouldn't eat most kinds of bread, cake, pancakes, waffles, cookies, muffins, pizza, and so on. They could substitute things made with other kinds of flour, like corn flour, which is used to make corn tortillas and corn chips. Or they could eat things not made from flour at all, such as french fries or rice.

Pages 12–14

OSF: Gelatin is made of long, thin protein strands. When cold water was added to the gelatin, the gelatin trapped the water between its strands, and swelled. The swollen gelatin formed the gumdrop.

1. Most people like candy because it's sweet.
2. A salt solution is salt dissolved in water.
3. Answers will vary. Sample answers: rubies, sapphires, emeralds, aquamarines, topaz, and garnets.
4. Answers to first question will vary. Sample answers: X rays can be used to take pictures of a person's bones and teeth, and to scan luggage (at airports). Answers to second question will vary. Sample answers: light rays, gamma rays, cosmic rays, ultraviolet rays, and infrared rays.
5. Answers will vary.

Pages 15–17

OSF: Milk contains proteins. When acids, like vinegar, react with milk, the proteins clump together to form *casein.* Lumps of casein are called curds. The remaining liquid is called whey.

1. Answers will vary. Sample answers: salad, coleslaw, sauerkraut, cabbage soup, corned beef and cabbage, and stuffed cabbage.
2. Grapefruit juice would make the indicator turn pink. Like oranges and lemons, grapefruits contain acid.
3. Cabbage was given this name because it's big and round, like a head.
4. Answers will vary. Sample answers: People should wear goggles, protective clothes, and gloves to handle sulfuric acid. If acid spills on someone, he or she should quickly wash it off with water.
5. People test their tank water with indicators because tropical fish get sick in acidic or basic water. The fish need neutral water. Answers to second question will vary. Sample answer: People could use indicators to test their drinking water or swimming pool water.

Pages 18–19

OSF: The blueberries contain *pigments,* or colored substances, that make them look blue. Some of the pigments in the blueberries *dissolve,* or break up, in water. This makes the water turn reddish-purple.

1. Answers will vary. Sample answers: apples (red, yellow, green), pears (brown and green), and plums (purple and red).
2. Answers will vary. Sample answers: to color clothes, hair, bodies, pottery, and ornaments.
3. Answers will vary. Sample answers: You could scratch a message into mud or sand with a stick; you could use rice or gravel to spell out words; you could dip your finger into paint and write a message.
4. Answers will vary. At the present time, people can't be made invisible.
5. Answers will vary. Sample answers: You could use a code that substitutes numbers for letters. For example, 1 = A, 2 = B, 3 = C, and so on. You could substitute one word or phrase for another. For example, blue = meet me; sweater = park; pants = seven o'clock. (Secret message: *Wear your blue sweater and pants tonight.* Meaning: *Meet me at the park at seven o'clock.*)

Pages 20–21

OSF: The bubbles in the soda are carbon dioxide gas. Carbon dioxide is lighter than the liquid in the soda, so the bubbles rise to the surface. When you add raisins, carbon dioxide bubbles collect on the raisins and raise them to the surface. At the surface the bubbles break, and the raisins sink. This happens again and again, until the carbon dioxide is gone.

1. Answers will vary. Sample answers: air, oxygen, nitrogen, water vapor, and helium.
2. Soda that has lost its gas bubbles is called flat soda. Most people don't like it.
3. A whale has a water spout.
4. The acid and base in baking powder combine to produce carbon dioxide gas. The expanding gas is trapped in the cake, and makes it rise.
5. Muscles and other parts of the body are made of protein. DNA, found in our cells, controls what we look like and how our bodies work.

Pages 22–23

OSF: The screw gets coated with a layer of copper, or becomes *copper plated.* When the dull pennies were soaked in the vinegar–salt bath, copper oxide dissolved off them. The liquid in the bowl then contained free copper particles. The free copper particles coated the screw.

1. Metals include aluminum, iron, lead, tin, gold, silver, bronze, and steel.
2. Answers will vary. Sample answers: aluminum foil, scissors, coins, soda cans, appliances (refrigerator, washing machine, dryer), eating utensils, keys, and pots and pans.
3. The pennies would get clean, because any weak acid will work.
4. Some examples of corroding metals are rusty iron nails (red), tarnished silver platters (black), and corroded brass trumpets (green).
5. Scientists think acid rain harms the environment by hurting crops, forests, and lakes, and by damaging buildings and other structures.

Pages 24–25

OSF: The fruits left at room temperature were browner than the fruits in the refrigerator. This happened because the chemicals in fruits react with oxygen more slowly at cold temperatures than at room temperature.

1. A bitten apple or banana would turn brown, because the bite would damage the cells.
2. Answers to first question will vary. You can keep the salad looking fresh by dipping the fruits in lemon juice, and keeping the salad cold.
3. Some other vitamins are A, B, D, E, and K. People need vitamins for their bodies to work right.
4. Answers will vary.
5. Most of the oxygen in the Earth's atmosphere is produced by plants. The other planets in the solar system have no plants, so they have little or no oxygen in their atmospheres.

Pages 26–27

OSF: The raisins swelled because of osmosis. The cells of raisins contain solutions of sugar, proteins, and other substances, dissolved in water. The plain water contained fewer particles than the solution in the raisin cells, so water moved into the raisins, and they swelled.

1. Cooks soak raisins to make them softer and plumper.
2. Soft drinks contain flavoring, sugar, coloring, and other substances, dissolved in water.
3. Osmosis is occurring when the roots of plants take up water from the soil.
4. Answers to first question will vary. Sample answers: frying, mashing, baking, roasting, boiling, and covering with sauce—like cheese sauce or gravy. Answers to second question will vary.
5. Salting keeps bacteria, which spoil food, from growing. The bacteria *dehydrate,* or lose their water, and die.

Pages 28–29

OSF: The plain chicken broth is the cloudiest because it has the most bacteria. The salted chicken broth is less cloudy, because salt inhibits the growth of bacteria. The chicken broth with vinegar is the least cloudy, because vinegar inhibits the growth of bacteria even better than salt.

1. Answers will vary. Sample answers: sandwiches and hamburgers.
2. Answers will vary. Sample answers: colds, the flu, chicken pox, strep throat, polio, measles, ear infections, and Lyme disease.
3. Answers will vary. Sample answers: eggs, beets, peppers, onions, peaches, pears, watermelon rind, and zucchini.
4. It's important for the environment because it prevents dead plants and animals from piling up. It also returns the *molecules,* or particles, of the dead plants and animals to nature.
5. Answers will vary. Sample answers: cook meat over a fire; put the food into a cold stream; bury the food in the snow; sun-dry some of the fruits and vegetables.

Pages 30–31

OSF: The papers have the same colors as the mottled milk. This happens because the milk and food coloring are *absorbed,* or drawn into, the spaces between the paper fibers.

1. Milk contains protein and calcium, which your body needs to grow.
2. People use food coloring to add color to food and other things. Second part of answer will vary. Sample answers: to make colorful cake frosting; to make colorful candies; to color Easter eggs; for arts and crafts—like homemade clay.
3. Food coloring *would* diffuse through water.
4. Answers will vary. Sample answers: Molecules of perfume or food diffuse through air, and people smell them. Molecules of smoke diffuse through air, and people see them.
5. Answers will vary.

Pages 32–33

OSF: At first, air pressure pushing on the water in the container was the same on the top and bottom. Water flowed out the bottom hole because of gravity. When you put your finger on the top hole, you stopped air from getting in. The air pressure under the container was then strong enough to keep the water from flowing out.

1. Water pressure is the "pushing force" of water molecules.
2. You're likely to notice air pressure when it's windy outside, and fast-moving air pushes on you.
3. Answers will vary. Sample answers: to control flooding; to make electricity with water power; to make the water deeper for boats; to supply irrigation water for crops; to make reservoirs for drinking water.
4. The capsized cup experiment wouldn't work on the Moon, because the Moon has no air and, therefore, no air pressure. The Moon does have enough gravity to pull the liquid down out of the cup.
5. Answers will vary.

Pages 34–35

OSF: The juice tastes sweetest on the front of the tongue because the taste buds for sweet flavors are located there. Taste buds for salty flavors are also near the front of the tongue; taste buds for sour flavors are on the sides of the tongue; and taste buds for bitter flavors are on the back of the tongue.

1. When our nose is stuffed, we can't smell our food very well. This makes the food taste funny.
2. Answers will vary. Sample answers: Cave dwellers probably ate nuts, fruits, seeds, some leaves and roots, and meat cooked over fires. Most of their food probably tasted different from ours because it was very fresh, had few spices and no additives, and was prepared in ways we don't often use anymore.
3. Answers will vary. Sample answers: vanilla and chocolate ice cream, regular and cheese flavor tortilla chips, sliced turkey and sliced ham, and strawberry and cherry Jell-O.
4. Answers will vary. Sample answers: Not everyone has the same favorite foods, because people come from different places, eat different things, and have different tastes.
5. Answers will vary.

Pages 36–37

OSF: The sound waves from your voice made the paper towel vibrate. The vibrating paper towel made the pepper bounce around. Some notes made the paper towel vibrate more than others, and caused the pepper to bounce higher.

1. Answers will vary. Sample answers: clarinets, saxophones, flutes, harmonicas, and recorders.
2. You *read* a book.
3. A song is a tune, with words, that you sing. Answers to second question will vary.
4. When guitar strings vibrate, they make the air around them vibrate. This creates a sound wave. The hollow body of the guitar vibrates also. This makes the sound wave louder. Answers to second question will vary. Sample answers: banjos, ukuleles, violins, cellos, harps, and pianos.
5. Plant parts include leaves, roots, fruits, flowers, and seeds. People use plant parts for food. For example, lettuce is made of leaves, celery stalks are stems, carrots are roots, broccoli is made of flowers, apples are fruits, and sunflower seeds are seeds. People also use plants—such as dried grasses—to make thatch huts and baskets.

Pages 38–39

OSF: The eggshell domes were able to support several books. This happened because domes are very strong shapes. When a force pushes down on a dome, the force is spread out over the dome's entire curved surface. No single point on the dome must withstand the force by itself. For this reason, domes are sometimes used for large structures, like indoor sports stadiums.

1. Answers will vary. Some very tall buildings are the Sears Tower in Chicago, the World Trade Center in New York, and City Hall in Toronto, Canada.
2. Our bones and muscles help us stand up straight.
3. Answers will vary. Sample answers: concrete for the foundation, wood or steel beams for the framework, plywood for the inside walls, bricks or cement blocks for the outside walls, wiring for electricity, pipes for plumbing, glass for windows, shingles for the roof, and so on.
4. 1 dozen eggs is 12 eggs. 1½ dozen eggs is 18 eggs. 2 dozen eggs is 24 eggs.
5. Answers will vary.

Pages 40–41

OSF: The center cookie on the left looks bigger than the center cookie on the right, but they're really the same size. This is an *optical illusion,* a picture that fools us. Optical illusions trick us because we "see" what we expect to see. In this case, we automatically compare the size of each center cookie with the cookies around it. The center cookie on the left is surrounded by small cookies, so it looks larger than it is, and vice versa.

1. Cameras are used to take photographs.
2. Answers will vary. Sample answers: Thaumatropes could be made from pictures of a duck and a pond, flowers and a vase, a car and a garage, and a fish and a fishbowl.
3. Answers will vary. Sample answers: video games, plastic toys of all kinds, Hot Wheels vehicles, toy airplanes, Barbie dolls, Star Wars toys, Rugrats toys, and remote control cars.
4. Answers will vary.
5. Answers will vary. Some sample answers: Freezing people in the Arctic might think they see a warm fire; hungry people on a barren prairie might think they see food.

Pages 42–43

OSF: Yogurt and cheese are made by adding harmless bacteria to milk. As the bacteria grow, solid chunks called *curds,* and liquid called *whey,* form. To make yogurt, the curds and whey are mixed together. To make soft cheese, the whey is drained off. To make hard cheese, the whey is drained off and the curds are dried. When you drain whey from yogurt, you make soft cheese.

1. The paddle breaks the membranes on the fat blobs, so they can clump together to form butter.
2. Answers will vary. Sample answers: Foods made with butter include cookies, cakes, buttered popcorn, and buttered toast. Foods made with milk include pudding, yogurt, hot chocolate, ice cream, cream soups, and cream sauces. Foods made with cheese include cheeseburgers, grilled cheese sandwiches, pizza, lasagna, and nachos.
3. A dairy farm has cows, and produces milk. Answers to second question will vary. Sample answers: crop farms (corn, wheat, soybeans, potatoes, tomatoes, and so on), poultry farms (chickens, turkeys, geese), fur farms (mink), ostrich farms, and deer farms.
4. Mammals are warm-blooded, have hair, and give birth to live babies (they don't lay eggs). Second part of answer will vary. Sample answers: ocean mammals include whales and dolphins; land mammals include people, dogs, cats, pigs, and elephants; flying mammals include bats and "flying" squirrels (these actually glide rather than fly).
5. Answers will vary.

Pages 44–45

OSF: Salt lowers the melting point of ice, so the ice around the string melted. However, the ice cube was very cold, so a little water quickly refroze and trapped the string. You were then able to lift the ice cube with the string.

1. A person feels chilly because heat flows from his or her body to the air.
2. People sprinkle salt on icy roads to make the ice melt more quickly.
3. Answers will vary. Sample answers: rivers, streams, currents, blood, wind, lava, glaciers, traffic, electric currents, snow (avalanche), mud (mud slide), and rocks (landslide).
4. Most of the heat on the Earth's surface comes from the sun. Outer space is much colder than Earth because outer space is not warmed by the sun.
5. Answers will vary.

Pages 46–47

OSF: The balloon got smaller. This happened because the air inside the balloon cooled and contracted.

1. Answers will vary. Sample answers: *Everything* in the kitchen is made of matter, including the refrigerator, stove, oven, toaster, microwave, fruits, vegetables, bread, snacks, and so on.
2. The water would freeze and expand, and the bottle would crack.
3. Steam is water vapor gas—the "gas form" of water.
4. Most of the ice on Earth is found in the Arctic and Antarctic. Answers to second question will vary. Sample answers: Ice is used for cooling drinks, ice skating, ice hockey, making homemade ice cream, making snow cones, keeping food cold in coolers, soothing injuries, and lowering fevers.
5. Answers to first question will vary. Sample answers: People could melt the ice, to get water for drinking, cooking, and growing plants. Water (which is made of oxygen and hydrogen) could be broken up to make oxygen for breathing. Answers to second question will vary.

Pages 48–49

OSF: The lid containing ice began to drip water first. This happened because the water in both jars evaporated to form water vapor. As water vapor cools, it condenses to form water drops. The ice-filled lid was colder than the other lid, so water drops formed there first and dripped down.

1. Seawater contains large amounts of salt, and fresh water doesn't.
2. Answers will vary. Sample answers: bathing, swimming, boating, flushing toilets, watering plants, and cooling car and truck engines.
3. Countries around Israel are Egypt, Jordan, and Syria. Countries around Kuwait are Iraq and Saudi Arabia.
4. Irrigation is a method of watering crops using man-made devices, like sprinklers and hoses.
5. When there's a drought, crops and wild animals die. Answers to second question will vary. Sample answers: taking quick showers or shallow baths, watering houseplants with used bath water, shutting off faucets when you're brushing your teeth, not washing cars, and not watering the lawn.

Pages 50–51

OSF: You can't pick up the apple without falling over. This happens because you aren't able to adjust your center of gravity. Normally, when you bend over, the bottom of your body moves back. Your center of gravity moves to a spot over your feet, and you can balance. In this experiment, the wall stopped you from moving back. You couldn't shift your center of gravity, so you began to fall over.

1. A baseball glove is not the same on both sides, so its center of gravity would not be in the exact center.
2. The straw would be the same on both sides, so its center of gravity would be in the middle.
3. Answers will vary. Sample answers: cent, tent, got, yet, give, tear, feet, far, and car.
4. Answers to first question will vary. Sample answers: pieces of spaghetti, boxes of tissue, bottles of ketchup, picture frames, ice-cream sandwiches, sunglasses, blocks, sofas, beds, and most animals (turtles, frogs, monkeys). Answers to second question will vary. Sample answers: balls, bubbles, cans of vegetables, plastic cups, daisies, sunflowers, jellyfish, bicycle tires, flower pots, and mushrooms.
5. The tower shaped like a pole will fall over more easily. This happens because the pyramid-shaped tower has a heavy bottom; its center of gravity is close to the ground. The pole-shaped tower is similar on both ends; its center of gravity is close to the middle.

Pages 52–53

OSF: The water particles at the surface of the glass linked together, and formed a strong, stretchy "skin" across the top of the water. This is called *surface tension.* The raisins you dropped in pushed aside some water, which rose to form a bulge on top. The water's "skin" stretched as the water rose, but finally broke when there were too many raisins in the glass. That's when the water overflowed.

1. The level of water in the bathtub rises, because your body displaces some water.
2. Another device used to weigh things is a *scale.*
3. Six inches of ruler are on either side of the pencil.
4. A shape with three equal sides is a triangle, with four equal sides is a square, and with five equal sides is a pentagon. Answers to last question will vary. Sample answers: cone, rectangle, circle, crescent, cylinder, pyramid, cube, octagon, heart, and diamond.
5. Answers will vary. Sample answer: You could throw a bunch of rocks down the well. The rocks would displace some water, and the level of water in the well would rise.

Pages 54–55

OSF: Oil is liquid fat. Water doesn't mix with fat, so the water didn't wash the oil off your hands. Dishwashing soap, however, helps water mix with fat and lets water wash off the oil–soap mixture.

1. Answers will vary.
2. Answers will vary. Sample answers: at, bat, brat, cat, chat, flat, gnat, hat, mat, pat, rat, sat, spat, splat, that, and vat.
3. Answers will vary. Sample answers: Foods that contain proteins include meats, eggs, milk, nuts, and beans. Foods that contain starches include bread, potatoes, corn, rice, and cereals.
4. Answers will vary. Sample answers: whales, walruses, seals, manatees, and penguins. Blubber is used for food and oil (for lanterns).
5. Answers will vary. Sample answers: Our bodies use fats for energy, to help build body parts, and to make chemicals that help control body functions.

Pages 56–57

OSF: The grape doesn't keep moving in a circle. It moves in a straight line. This happens because every object in the universe has inertia. Inertia makes a moving object travel in a straight line, unless something changes its direction. The ring forced the grape to move in a circle. As soon as the ring was lifted, inertia made the grape move in a straight line.

1. A child on a bicycle would experience centrifugal force when he or she rounded a corner, made a U-turn, or rode in a circle.
2. A carousel is a ride that goes around and around. It often has figures of horses, or other animals, for people to sit on. Carousels are usually found at fairs and amusement parks.
3. The grape in the twirling soda bottle moved in a circle because the bottle was round. If the bottle was flattened—like a salad dressing bottle—the grape wouldn't move in a circle.
4. Gravity is present all the time. Gravity pulls objects down, toward Earth. Centrifugal force is present only when objects move in a circle. Centrifugal force makes objects push out, away from the center of the circle.
5. Answers to first question will vary. Sample answers: Other scientists who did important work include chemists, like Marie and Pierre Curie, who discovered new chemical elements; doctors, like Jonas Salk and Albert Sabin, who developed polio vaccines; biologists, like Rachel Carson, who worked to improve the environment; inventors, like Alexander Graham Bell, who invented the telephone; and physicists, like Richard Feynman, who made new discoveries about tiny particles in the universe. Answers to second question will vary.

Pages 58–59

OSF: The fast-moving stream of air between the balloons had lower pressure than the still air on the outside of the balloons. The higher pressure of the outside air pushed the balloons together.

1. Answers will vary. Sample answers: breathing, inflating tires, inflating balloons, sailing boats, whistling, playing flutes (and other wind instruments), and moving pinwheels and windmills.
2. A bird's wings are similar to an airplane's wings. Birds do use Bernoulli's principle to fly.
3. Helium balloons don't use Bernoulli's principle to fly. They fly because helium gas is lighter than air, so it rises.
4. A Swiss scientist comes from Switzerland.
5. Orville and Wilbur Wright built and flew the first airplane. The airplane had wings and used Bernoulli's principle.

Glossary

Air pressure: The pushing force of air. Air is made up of many molecules that bounce around and push on everything.

Atom: The smallest particle of matter, the building block of everything around us.

Bernoulli's principle: The fact that fast-moving air has less pressure than slow-moving or still air.

Biology: The study of life.

Centripetal force: A force that pulls a whirling object toward the center of the circle it's whirling around.

Chemical properties: Characteristics or traits of substances. A chemical's properties help scientists predict the way it will react in different situations.

Chemistry: The study of materials and how they interact.

Condensation: The process of gas becoming liquid.

Dehydration: The removal of water from a substance.

Diffusion: The process of molecules spreading out from a place where they are crowded to a place where they are less so.

Earth's atmosphere: The hundreds of miles of air that surround the Earth, covering it like a blanket.

Evaporation: The process of liquid becoming gas.

Gravity: The force that pulls any two objects together because of their mass. The Earth pulls everything toward its center with the force of gravity.

Indicator: A substance that changes color in the presence of an acid or base.

Inertia: The force that resists change in movement. Things at rest will tend to stay at rest; things that are moving will tend to keep moving until another force comes into play.

Matter: Any substance that has weight and can be perceived by the senses.

Microbes: Tiny life-forms such as bacteria, viruses, and some fungi. We cannot see microbes unless we use a microscope.

Molecule: The smallest particle of a substance that still has that substance's characteristics. A molecule is formed when two or more atoms link together.

Physics: The study of how energy interacts with mass.

Polymer: A large, chainlike molecule.

Proteins: A group of complex compounds that are found in all living things.

Saturated: When a substance has been filled to its capacity.

Solutions: Solids that have broken up, or dissolved in liquids.

Index